HAMILTON

AN ADULT COLORING BOOK

A POST HILL PRESS BOOK

Hamilton: An Adult Coloring Book
© 2016 by Post Hill Press
All Rights Reserved

ISBN: 978-1-68261-225-5

Interior layout by Greg Johnson, Textbook Perfect
Some artwork elements are used courtesy of vecteezy.com.

Post Hill
PRESS
Post Hill Press
posthillpress.com

Published in the United States of America

2 3 4 5 6 7 8 9 10

THE EXACT DATE OF ALEXANDER HAMILTON'S BIRTH IS UNKNOWN; IT WAS AROUND JANUARY 11, IN EITHER 1755 OR 1757. HE WAS BORN IN THE BRITISH WEST INDIES TO UNWED PARENTS, A SCOTSMAN AND A DAUGHTER OF A FRENCH PHYSICIAN. HIS FATHER ABANDONED THE YOUNG FAMILY WHEN HAMILTON WAS JUST TEN YEARS OLD, AND HIS MOTHER UNEXPECTEDLY DIED OF AN UNKNOWN ILLNESS TWO YEARS LATER. HAMILTON TOOK A JOB AT A ST. CROIX COUNTING HOUSE WHERE HIS WORK ETHIC AND INTELLECT SHONE THROUGH. THE OWNER WAS SUFFICIENTLY IMPRESSED THAT HE FUNDED HAMILTON'S EDUCATION AT KING'S COLLEGE, NOW KNOWN AS COLUMBIA UNIVERSITY.

ALEXANDER HAMILTON ATTENDED KING'S COLLEGE (NOW
COLUMBIA UNIVERSITY) FROM THE FALL OF 1773 TO 1776. HE
FLOURISHED IN THE ACADEMIC ENVIRONMENT, PURSUING
AN ACCELERATED PROGRAM, AND ENGAGING IN HEATED
POLITICAL DEBATES. HE ALSO PUBLISHED ESSAYS IN DEFENSE OF
THE COLONISTS WHO REBELLED AGAINST EXCESSIVE BRITISH
RULE. HE WROTE, "TO USURP DOMINION OVER A PEOPLE...OR TO
GRASP AT A MORE EXTENSIVE POWER THAN THEY ARE WILLING
TO ENTRUST, IS TO VIOLATE THAT LAW OF NATURE, WHICH GIVES
EVERY MAN A RIGHT TO HIS PERSONAL LIBERTY."

IT IS ONE THING TO SUPPORT A CAUSE THROUGH POLITICAL WRITINGS, AND IT'S SOMETHING VERY DIFFERENT TO PUT YOUR PERSONAL SAFETY AT RISK FOR THAT CAUSE. WHILE STILL A STUDENT AT KING'S COLLEGE, ALEXANDER HAMILTON JOINED THE LOCAL MILITIA IN SUPPORT OF THE AMERICAN REVOLUTION. BY MARCH OF 1776, HE WITHDREW FROM SCHOOL AND BECAME THE CAPTAIN OF AN ARTILLERY COMPANY, DEDICATING HIS FULL ATTENTION TO THE CAUSE OF LIBERTY. HE FOUGHT IN THE VERY FIRST BATTLES OF THE REVOLUTION AT LEXINGTON AND CONCORD.

IN 1777, GEORGE WASHINGTON INVITED ALEXANDER HAMILTON TO JOIN HIS STAFF. HAMILTON ASSUMED THE RESPONSIBILITIES OF LIEUTENANT COLONEL, AND HE EARNED THE RESPECT OF WASHINGTON DURING THEIR TWENTY-TWO YEARS OF SERVICE TOGETHER. WASHINGTON BECAME A TRUSTED MENTOR FOR HAMILTON WHO IN TURN GREW INTO A VITAL ADVISOR TO OUR FIRST PRESIDENT.

Alexander Hamilton always had a strong desire to actively fight in the American Revolution, but George Washington consistently overlooked him when it came time to appoint new commanders in the field. Their close relationship grew fractured as Hamilton's frustration festered, until he finally resigned his post on Washington's staff. Shared values and goals led to a reconciliation that allowed Hamilton to join the Battle at Yorktown, the last major offensive on American soil that resulted in the capture of the British commander and an end to the conflict.

ALEXANDER HAMILTON AND ELIZABETH
SCHUYLER WERE MARRIED IN DECEMBER
1780. UNLIKE ALEXANDER, ELIZABETH
CAME FROM AN ARISTOCRATIC NEW
YORK FAMILY WHO SHARED STRONG TIES
TO GEORGE WASHINGTON AND THE
REVOLUTION. HAMILTON'S NEW BRIDE
BECAME HIS CLOSEST CONFIDANT, AIDING
HIS POLITICAL CAREER. THEY HAD EIGHT
CHILDREN TOGETHER.

IN THE LATE 18TH CENTURY, ADMISSION TO THE STATE BAR
TYPICALLY REQUIRED A THREE-YEAR LEGAL INTERNSHIP FOR
STUDY AND PREPARATION. HOWEVER, ALEXANDER HAMILTON
DID NOT HAVE PATIENCE FOR THE DELAY. BECAUSE HE WAS A
FORMER MEMBER OF GEORGE WASHINGTON'S STAFF, THE NEW
YORK SUPREME COURT GRANTED HAMILTON A SPECIAL WAIVER
TO BYPASS THE INTERNSHIP PROCESS. WITH JUST THREE MONTHS
OF INTENSE STUDY, IN 1882 HE PASSED THE BAR EXAM AND
COULD PRACTICE LAW IN NEW YORK.

After earning his law license, Alexander Hamilton shifted his attention to the needs of the fledgling nation. He recognized that financial hardships were the greatest hurdles to a successful government, and he began to advocate for a centralized bank and the power of Congress to levy taxes. In 1782, Hamilton was appointed Receiver of Continental Taxes in New York, and that same year he was elected to Congress as a representative of New York State. It would be the first of his two terms in Congress. He went on to become an architect and signer of the United States Constitution, serve as our first Secretary of the Treasury, and help establish the Federalist Party.

ALEXANDER HAMILTON IS CONSIDERED
TO BE THE FATHER OF AMERICA'S
NATIONAL BANKING SYSTEM. UNDER
HIS LEADERSHIP, THE BANK OF THE
UNITED STATES WAS ESTABLISHED IN
1791, A CENTRAL ENTITY THAT WOULD
REGULATE AND CONTROL THE NATION'S
WEALTH AND FINANCES.

ALEXANDER HAMILTON LOVED KNOWLEDGE
ALMOST AS MUCH AS HE LOVED FREEDOM. HE
SUPPORTED EDUCATIONAL ENDEAVORS AND
INSTITUTIONS THROUGHOUT HIS LIFE. HE
SERVED ON THE NEW YORK BOARD OF REGENTS,
RESURRECTED HIS ALMA MATER KING'S COLLEGE,
HELPED ESTABLISH THE OLDEST CHARTER SCHOOL
IN NEW YORK, AND PROVIDED LEGAL SERVICES
TO THE AFRICAN FREE SCHOOL. THESE EFFORTS
DEMONSTRATE THE POWERFUL ROLE EDUCATION
PLAYED IN HAMILTON'S LIFE.

ALEXANDER HAMILTON BELIEVED IN THE VIRTUES OF A STRONG FEDERAL GOVERNMENT. HE AUTHORED THE ANNAPOLIS RESOLUTION, WHICH FORMALLY ESTABLISHED WHAT HAS BECOME KNOWN AS THE CONSTITUTIONAL CONVENTION. IT WAS HERE THE INITIAL STEPS WERE TAKEN TO REPLACE THE ARTICLES OF CONFEDERATION WITH THE UNITED STATES CONSTITUTION.

In 1787, fifty-five delegates met at the Philadelphia State House to draft the Constitution of the United States. The process took more than four months, and the men often met six days a week. Alexander Hamilton was only in his thirties, but he was one of the most influential delegates to shape the Constitution.

THE

FEDERALIST:

A COLLECTION OF

E S S A Y S,

WRITTEN IN FAVOUR OF THE

NEW CONSTITUTION,

AS AGREED UPON BY THE

FEDERAL CONVENTION,

SEPTEMBER 17, 1787.

IN TWO VOLUMES.
VOL. I.

NEW-YORK:
PRINTED AND SOLD BY JOHN TIEBOUT,
No. 358 PEARL STREET.
1799.

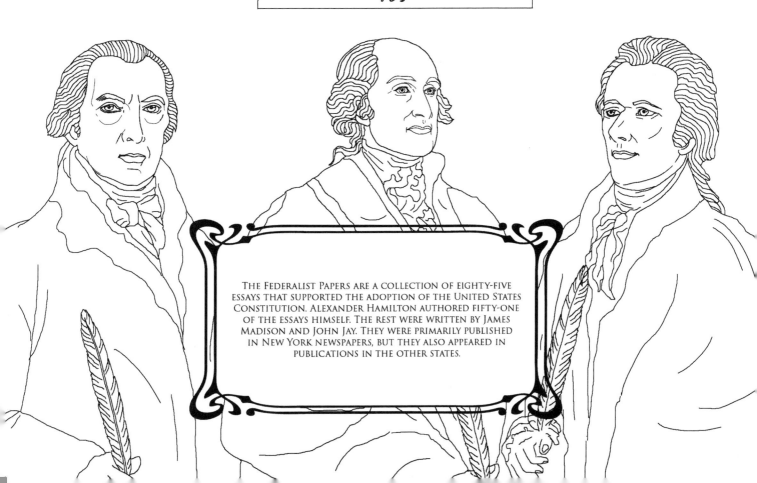

THE FEDERALIST PAPERS ARE A COLLECTION OF EIGHTY-FIVE
ESSAYS THAT SUPPORTED THE ADOPTION OF THE UNITED STATES
CONSTITUTION. ALEXANDER HAMILTON AUTHORED FIFTY-ONE
OF THE ESSAYS HIMSELF. THE REST WERE WRITTEN BY JAMES
MADISON AND JOHN JAY. THEY WERE PRIMARILY PUBLISHED
IN NEW YORK NEWSPAPERS, BUT THEY ALSO APPEARED IN
PUBLICATIONS IN THE OTHER STATES.

HAMILTON

George Washington appointed Alexander Hamilton to be the first Secretary of the Treasury. He served in this capacity from 1789 to 1795, and his first major undertaking was to repay the nation's war debt. While some believed the United States didn't have to recognize the debt incurred during the revolution, Hamilton saw repayment as an opportunity to establish the credibility and good will of the new nation. During his tenure, he went on to create the basis of our modern financial systems, established the Bank of the United States, and developed a system of tariffs to provide funding to the government.

As the Secretary of the Treasury, Alexander Hamilton began to put in place his long-held vision for a robust financial system. A cornerstone of this system was a national currency. Under his leadership, Congress passed The Coinage Act in April of 1792. It authorized the construction of the mint, the first federal building built pursuant to the Constitution.

ALEXANDER HAMILTON KNEW THAT THE BEST REVENUE STREAM FOR THE NEW UNITED STATES OF AMERICA WOULD COME BY SEA IN THE FORM OF TARIFFS. AS THE SECRETARY OF THE TREASURY, HE ALSO RECOGNIZED THAT PIRACY AND SMUGGLING WERE HUGE BARRIERS TO COLLECTING THOSE TARIFFS. HIS SOLUTION WAS TO COMMISSION A SMALL FLEET OF TEN CUTTERS THAT WOULD PATROL THE EAST COAST AND ENSURE PROPER ENFORCEMENT OF THE LAWS. THESE BOATS WOULD SOON BE KNOWN AS THE REVENUE CUTTER SERVICE, THE PRECURSOR TO OUR MODERN DAY COAST GUARD.

In an effort to pay down the American Revolution war debt, Alexander Hamilton initiated a tax on whiskey. It was the first tax imposed on a domestic product, and it was wildly unpopular. Farmers on the western frontier were particularly well organized in their opposition; they had been accustomed to distilling their surplus crops and using the liquor as a type of currency. When the U.S. marshal arrived to serve writs on the distillers who failed to pay the tax, five hundred armed men tarred and feathred the tax inspector. In response, George Washington summoned some thirteen thousand militia men to quell the uprising. While no armed conflict ensued, the incident demonstrated that the national government could—and would—suppress violent challenges to its laws.

KNOWN AS A PROLIFIC WRITER WHO HAD A SPECIAL WAY WITH WORDS, ALEXANDER HAMILTON HELPED GEORGE WASHINGTON CRAFT HIS FAREWELL ADDRESS. THE ADDRESS ANNOUNCED THAT WASHINGTON WOULD NOT SEEK A THIRD TERM IN OFFICE, AND SERVED AS AN OPPORTUNITY TO REFLECT ON THE PAST AND OFFER A VISION OF A BRIGHT FUTURE FOR AMERICA.

POLITICAL SCANDAL IS NEARLY AS OLD AS THE REPUBLIC ITSELF, AND EVEN ALEXANDER HAMILTON COULD NOT ESCAPE ITS VICIOUS GRIP. IN 1797, WHAT STARTED OUT AS AN INVESTIGATION INTO ALLEGATIONS OF FINANCIAL IMPROPRIETY TURNED INTO THE DISCOVERY OF AN EXTRAMARITAL AFFAIR BETWEEN HAMILTON AND MARIA REYNOLDS. THROUGH THE COURSE OF THE INVESTIGATION, HIS LOVE LETTERS FOUND THEIR WAY INTO THE HANDS OF THOMAS JEFFERSON, ONE OF HAMILTON'S FIERCEST POLITICAL OPPONENTS. JEFFERSON GAVE THE LETTERS TO A LOCAL PUBLISHER, AND SOON THE PRIVATE WRITINGS WERE IN PRINT FOR ALL OF HIS FELLOW CITIZENS TO READ. HAMILTON ISSUED A PUBLIC APOLOGY THAT SOME COMMENDED FOR ITS HONESTY, BUT HIS POLITICAL CAREER WOULD NEVER AGAIN BE THE SAME.

In 1798, shortly after leaving his post as Secretary of the Treasury, George Washington called on Alexander Hamilton again – this time to lead the national armed forces. As Major General, Alexander Hamilton commanded the forces during a volatile time with France. With a new regime in place after the French Revolutionary Wars, the United States stopped paying its war debt, citing the fact that it was owed to the previous government. France retaliated with attacks on American shipping routes, and the two-year conflict led America to reestablish its navy and create the United States Marine Corps.

In 1880 Thomas Jefferson ran as a Democratic-Republican and defeated Federalist John Adams. But Jefferson was still left in a tie with fellow Republican Aaron Burr. Hamilton used his influence to endorse Jefferson, the lesser of two evils in his view. For Burr, it fed his growing resentment against Hamilton.

TRUE TO HIS BELIEF IN THE POWER OF THE
WRITTEN WORD, ALEXANDER HAMILTON
FOUNDED *THE NEW YORK EVENING POST*
ALONG WITH OTHER PROMINENT FEDERALISTS
IN 1801. *THE POST* WAS THE THIRTEENTH
NEWSPAPER TO BE CREATED IN THE UNITED
STATES, AND TODAY *THE NEW YORK POST* IS
AMERICA'S OLDEST DAILY NEWSPAPER.

IN 1801, OUTRAGED OVER CRITICISM DIRECTED AT HIS FATHER
DURING A FOURTH OF JULY SPEECH, HAMILTON'S SON PHILIP
CONFRONTED GEORGE I. EACKER IN A MANHATTAN THEATER
TO DEFEND HIS FATHER'S NAME. THE DISPUTE LED TO THE
CHALLENGE OF A DUEL WHICH ULTIMATELY TOOK PLACE IN
WEEHAWKEN, NEW JERSEY – THE SAME LOCATION WHERE
ALEXANDER HAMILTON WOULD LATER BE KILLED BY AARON
BURR. PHILIP DIED OF AN INFECTION WITHIN HOURS OF BEING
SHOT. HE WAS NINETEEN YEARS OLD.

In 1802, the Hamilton family moved into a newly built country house called The Grange. The home is located in St. Nicholas Park in New York and is known as the Hamilton Grange National Museum. It has been restored to its original condition, allowing visitors to step back to a time when Alexander Hamilton helped shape our nation.

After years of political jostling and personal insults, Alexander Hamilton and Aaron Burr stood facing each other on the dueling grounds of Weehawken, New Jersey – the same location where Hamilton's son Philip was shot three years prior. The confrontation was instigated by Burr, then the sitting Vice President of the United States. He saw political benefits from a potential victory, and though Hamilton sought to avoid the duel, he would ultimately choose to defend his honor. As shots rang out from the .56 caliber pistols, Hamilton was mortally wounded. He succumbed to his injuries the next day, July 12, 1804. Burr never held elected office again.

ALEXANDER HAMILTON
The CORPORATION of TRINITY CHURCH Has erected
In Testimony of their Respect
FOR
The PATRIOT of incorruptible INTEGRITY.
The SOLDIER of approved VALOUR.
The STATESMAN of consummate WISDOM:
Whose TALENTS and VIRTUES will be admired
Grateful Posterity:
Long after this MARBLE shall have moldered into
DUST.
He died July 12. 1804 Aged 47.

THE FUNERAL FOR ALEXANDER HAMILTON
WAS HELD ON JULY 14, 1804 AT TRINITY
CHURCH. THOUSANDS LINED THE STREETS
TO PAY THEIR RESPECTS AND MANY STILL
VISIT HIS GRAVESITE TODAY.

FEDERAL RESERVE NOTE

THE UNITED STATES OF AMERICA

FEDERAL RESERVE BANK OF BOSTON MASSACHUSETTS

A

TEN

HAMILTON

WILL PAY TO THE BEARER ON DEMAND

TEN DOLLARS

10

10

10

10

As the first Secretary of the Treasury and one of the most prominent Founding Fathers, Alexander Hamilton has appeared on the ten dollar bill since 1929. He is only one of two non-presidents to appear on United States paper currency, the other being Benjamin Franklin on the hundred dollar bill.

IT MAY BE HARD TO BELIEVE THAT THE MEMORY OF A MAN
COULD PERSIST FOR MORE THAN TWO HUNDRED YEARS WHEN
HIS CENTRAL ACHIEVEMENTS CENTERED ON ECONOMIC POLICY
AND POLITICAL PHILOSOPHY. BUT TODAY HAMILTON'S STORY
IS SEEN AS THE STORY OF AMERICA – AN IMMIGRANT WHOSE
TALENTS CONTRIBUTED TO BUILDING OUR GREAT NATION. HIS
POPULARITY HAS SKYROCKETED SINCE THE RELEASE OF THE
BLOCKBUSTER BROADWAY MUSICAL *HAMILTON*.

HAMILTON

THOUGH BORN IN THE WEST INDIES, ALEXANDER HAMILTON
ADOPTED NEW YORK AS HIS HOME. IN 1880, CARL CONRADS
WAS COMMISSIONED TO SCULPT A GRANITE STATUE OF THE
FOUNDING FATHER. TODAY IT STANDS IN NEW YORK CITY'S
CROWN JEWEL, CENTRAL PARK.

HAMILTON

THE LIFE-SIZE PORTRAIT OF ALEXANDER HAMILTON CREATED IN
1792 WHILE HE WAS SERVING AS SECRETARY OF THE TREASURY IS
CONSIDERED TO BE THE GREATEST KNOWN DEPICTION OF THE
FOUNDING FATHER. PAINTED BY RENOWNED REVOLUTIONARY-
ERA ARTIST JOHN TRUMBULL, THE PORTRAIT SHOWS A MAN WHO
EXHIBITS PRIDE, INTELLECT AND AN AVERSION FOR THE EXCESSES
OF LIFE.

COLORING BOOKS